LEAVING TRAUMA BEHIND

Turning a new Leaf

By:K.Moore

Book 3   **Volume 1**

Copyright © 2024 by K.Moore

All rights reserved. No part of this book may be used or reproduced in any form whatsoever without written permission except in the case of brief quotations in critical articles or reviews.

This book is a work of fiction. Names, characters, businesses, organizations, places, events and incidents either are the product of the author's imagination or are used fictitiously. Any resemblance to actual persons, living or dead, events, or locales is entirely coincidental.

For more information, or to book an event, contact :
relatablefictionwriting@gmail.com
http://www.relatablefictionwriting.com

Book design by Nakeia Davis
Cover design by Canva

ISBN - Paperback: 9798224940417

First Edition: May 2024

Prologue

We forgot to mention that Janette's 5th date happens to be a retired police chief. When the kidnapping came out at the table Michael Byrd wanted to help. Zeek asked him to take Janette home and wait in case Destiny came back looking for Harmony. That plan was followed and brought Janette and Michael together. Let's hope that all our characters can turn a new leaf and create new chapters as we leave trauma behind.

1

Race against time

While Zeek, Rashad and Max were searching for Christian and Camille, Destiny and Melody were over the state line in a warehouse with the kids tied up. Will you "Shut Up" Destiny yelled at Camille who was crying for her big brother. Stop yelling at my sister. She's only 11 months old and she's probably hungry Christian replied. He's right Melody stated: We both missed out on raising our children so we can't take our stress out on her.

Back at the house Janette was pacing the floor full of worry about her grandbabies. Michael was on the phone with the dispatcher to get as much information as possible on the situation. Janette couldn't take it anymore and called Kahlani to check on Malcolm. When her phone rang it startled Kahlani awake so she answered it without checking the caller i.d. Janette spoke as soon as the call connected, rolling off a list of questions. (1)How is Malcolm doing?(2) Is Harmony with you?(3) Have you heard from the boys yet?

Feeling a little drowsy Kahlani answered solemnly: (1) Malcolm is fine he'll be able to come home tomorrow(2) Harmony is here with us and she's been here since they brought him in(3) No I haven't heard from any of the boys yet. But while I have you on the phone let me ask you; Is Michael still there at the house with you? Girl:Yes he's on the phone getting everybody out there to find those babies. Janette he's a good man like your son don't let him get away.

I won't daughter but you know what I think I finally found the right man for me. I just got an idea; the boys need to find out how Destiny was able to escape from prison. Maybe we'll be able to find out where she took the kids. Kahlani got excited hearing the idea saying: that's a great idea, ask Michael to look into it. If he finds anything, call Zeek immediately so we can get this over with.

I will Lani, let me get off this phone and talk to Mike but I'll be in touch. After hanging up Janette made her way to the living room to find Michael ending a call with dispatch. Mike mind if I share something with you, Janette asked. Sure what's on your mind sugar Michael replied. Well the question is: Who and How did destiny escape from prison? Someone on the inside had to help her plan her escape that needed to be looked into. After hearing this idea Michael looked as if a lightbulb went off in his head.

2

New Search strategy

I know people that work at the prison she was housed in, let me look into something. This news excited Janette so much she replied "Alright" and turned to go into the kitchen. She made her way over to the microwave to heat up the food she brought home from their date. Janette could overhear the conversation Michael was having with the warden of the women's prison. After greetings were exchanged Michael asked for a list of the officers working the day Destiny escaped.

Give me a second to pull up that information for you, my friend Randall Spates answered. While my computer is loading let me ask you : why is this information so important to you Mike? Remember I told you I was going on a date tonight Michael asked. Yeah man I remember you telling me that Mike. Well the kids that Destiny kidnapped are my date's grandchildren Randall. Oh! well in that case let me take a closer look at this for you Randall replied. You won't believe this Mike but it seems Melody Stanton has escaped as well. The only guard on duty when they escaped was Jamal Reynolds. He claimed to have a family emergency when they escaped and hasn't been heard from since. Maybe he's aiding and abetting them in the kidnapping Michael replied concerned.

We need to find him and see what he knows regarding their whereabouts. Randall, we need to work fast. The youngest of those children is only 11 months old. I'll text you all the info I have on Reynolds and we'll both try to track him down. This is truly a race against time, but we'll get those kids home. I'm going to check some more things but like I said we'll get them home Randall stated.

I appreciate it Randall , my lady feels better and she can stop pacing the floor worried. I got you Mike don't worry, let's get off the phone and start this search party.Thanks again Randall, Mike stated gratefully then hung up the phone. Janette came out of the kitchen with worry and caution for what she might hear from his lips. Michael looked up and reached out his hand for her to take. Janette takes his hand and has a seat on the couch next to him.

Listen to me carefully Janette I'm working on getting those babies back OK. Don't worry your pretty little head off all night, go get some sleep for me. I got it from here. Janette stared at Michael for a second and leaned over to give him a kiss on the cheek. Then she headed upstairs to her room to lay down for the night. Michael spent the next 2 hours on the phone trying to track down Officer Jamal Reynolds.

After numerous calls Michael finally tracked down Reynolds applying for a job at the Sheriff Office over the state line in Virginia. Once Michael has him on the line the questioning begins. (1) Did you help those two girls escape?(2)Where are they and the kids?(3)Did they promise you anything in exchange for helping them?(4) Do you know Randall is looking for you?(5) Why'd you lie about having a family emergency?

Michael stepped out on the porch to listen clearly to Jamal's responses. (1)Yes I did help both of them escape.(2) They took the kids to a warehouse over the state line in North Carolina. (3)They didn't promise me anything,I got what I wanted while they were in custody.(4)I know Randall's looking for me, he called 4 times before you called.(5) Lastly;I lied to cover my tracks and get the girls out unseen.

3

Tracking down suspects

Michael looked at the phone stunned at what he just heard from Jamal. Then he asked Reynolds, You know you have to turn yourself in for aiding two fugitives? Reynolds solemnly replies: I'm aware and I will but you know applying for this job was just a coverup so I can lay low for awhile. Michael asked one last question before hanging up to call Randall back. Why would you go for a job in law enforcement after committing a crime one state away. I don't know how to answer that. Maybe it's because it's the only profession I know how to do. I understand that wholeheartedly now that I'm retired.

Before I let you go I need to give you some other info about this case. The girls have been in contact with Roger Williams to find a place to hide the kids. With this new information Michael knew now that Zeek, Max and Rashad needed more backup than expected then he hung up. Immediately calling Zeek to let him know we have to change the search plan. Frustrated and tired, Zeek answered his ringing phone without looking at it. Hello:Any news for me on my kids? Yes:son I have a lot of information for you and I need you to listen to me and don't overreact Michael said.

Zeek placed the call on speaker for Max and Rashad to hear the plan. Alright Chief what you got for us to work with so I can bring my kids home tonight. (1) Both Melody and Destiny escaped and they're together.(2)A guard from the prison (Jamal Reynolds)helped them escape.(3)They've been in contact with your dad, he gave them access to one of his warehouses in North Carolina.(4) The warden has U.S Marshals headed to Virginia to pick up Reynolds and bring him back. Zeek I need you to go see your dad and find out where that warehouse is.

If you'd like I'll call in some more help to get in the warehouse once you find out where it is. All three of the men were shocked to hear the information Michael relayed to them. Then Zeek cleared his throat and replied: I appreciate that Mike I'll be in touch when I come out of the prison. Alright son I'll let you get to it and I'm going to eat while your mom is sleeping. Another thing your wife said Malcolm has a concussion but he'll be able to come home tomorrow then he hung up.

Zeek never thought his father could be so hard headed as to keep interfering in his life. As he drove to the prison both

Max and Rashad were firing off questions in disbelief of the situation. Zeek was so angry he couldn't even respond to his friends in the car. Once he got to the prison Zeek completely zoned out as he went to the visitors room to speak to his father again. Once Roger walked in to see all three men sitting across from him, he nodded his head with a laugh and took a seat.

What do I owe the pleasure of this visit son I thought we were never to be around each other again.Zeek looked at each man next to him then at Roger and replied: Why are you helping Melody and Destiny disrupt my happiness again? Then Max asked: Where are the kids being held? Then Rashad followed up with the big question: Where is the warehouse located? Roger just sat there smiling at them, then he said simply: what's in it for me?

4

New Search Party

You get to continue living now tell me where my children are, was all Zeek had the energy to say to Roger. In turn Roger sat back and looked at his son and stated: they're over the state line in North Carolina in my warehouse , maybe they're already dead since you wouldn't give me what I want. I had your baby mamas go get them for me but you foiled the rest of the plan by showing up here tonight. So you telling us that you were going to escape and go abuse your own grandchildren, Max replied. Roger nodded his head in certainty that the information was correct.

Roger for the last time tell me where my kids are,Zeek yelled, slamming his hands on the table. Rashad handed Roger a notepad and a pen then told him to write it down since he wouldn't talk. Roger took the pen and started writing down directions to the warehouse, after each sentence he'd look up at Zeek who stared at him unflinching and unintimidated. When he was done Roger slid the notepad and pen over to his son with a smirk.

If you lying to me and I don't find my kids alive I will execute you myself personally in this prison. Rashad picked up the notepad and opened it to the first page finding detailed directions to the warehouse. Zeek then stood up and walked to the door without a word. As the three men got into the car Zeek called Michael with the information he had received from Roger. After giving Michael the detailed directions to the warehouse Michael responded by telling Zeek "I know where that is let me call the department out there to get you some backup". Thanks for all your help Chief. I really appreciate you, the guys and I are headed there now, Zeek responded.

Anytime Son let's get these babies home and I'll try to stop your mom from worrying because her pacing is making me dizzy. With a chuckle Zeek added "Good Luck with that man" then hung up. Michael called over to some old friends in Asher Township where the warehouse was located in North Carolina. Michael made it clear the urgency of the situation and the ages of the children involved. He also informed them that the two uncles and the father of the children are local Tennessee police headed there to bring them home. The officers told Mike they would be awaiting their arrival and had S.W.A.T headed to the warehouse.

While enroute to get the kids Kahlani called Zeek anxious for any information on her babies. I can't talk right now baby, I have to focus on the task at hand was all Zeek said before handing the phone to Max. Kahlani rambled off questions in hysteria: Max what's happening, where are the kids being held at, is there anything I can do to help get them home? Max took a deep breath and said: Lani all you need to do is relax. Roger just gave us directions of where Destiny and Melody are holding the kids. We're headed to Asher Township to get them and be ready for another court case. All Kahlani could say was OK and hang up.

In the warehouse Melody and Destiny sat staring at the still battered and bruised bodies of 11 yr old Christian and 11 month old Camille on the floor tied up. What should we do with them? Melody asked Destiny. We wait for Jamal to help us get rid of the bodies before the police close in. Just then the door to the warehouse opened to the site of Jamal.

5

Search is completed

Once he'd come into the warehouse and saw the bodies of the two children Jamal was appalled. What did you do to them? Are they dead or just unconscious was all he could say to both of them. I don't know Melody replied ; they haven't moved since Destiny fed them two hours ago. After checking the children's pulse Jamal found that Christian was barely alive and Camille was unconscious but alive. Then he looked up at Melody and asked where Destiny was at that moment?

She was upstairs making us something to eat while we waited for you. I'll go tell her you're here, Melody replied. Five minutes later the two ladies came down the stairs with plates of food in hand but Destiny had no reaction to the sight of the children. The sight of Jamal standing next to the children with his hands on his waist with a look of disgust made Destiny stop in her tracks. She approached him offering a plate of food to which he declined and roared:Do you know the police are out looking for these kids?

I know baby but as you can see they're resting so we won't be in any trouble, Destiny states. Woman do you not get it, we are wanted by the feds for this right here,Jamal roared. Don't be so worried baby, we've had them for 5 hours and there's no news bulletin being aired about them, Melody replied. You two are so stupid for this, how do you expect any man to take you back by kidnapping his kids and beating them. When this is over I never want to hear from either one of you again.

Before anyone could respond the door opened to reveal a S.W.A.T team of police led by Zeek, Max and Rashad. Zeek stood there in the doorway in a standoff position staring at Jamal,Destiny and Melody. Rashad and Max walked around them to look for the kids which were tied up and unconscious in the corner. Rashad yelled: we need to get them out of here fast they're barely alive man. Asher Township radioed for an ambulance for the children while taking the three suspects into custody. All Zeek had the energy to do was thank all the S.W.A.T members for helping find his children ashe walked to the ambulance to get in.

The look of worry and tiredness was evident on his face as he looked at his babies on the stretcher. Once at the hospital Rashad and Max sat with Zeek waiting for the doctor's report on the kids. Yo, Zeek do you want to call the girls and give them an update or wait til we talk to the doctors Max asked. Without looking up Zeek replied:Just wait I want to know what they did to my babies first before telling my wife anything. A minute later a doctor came into the waiting room. Doc, how are my niece and nephew doing? asked Rashad followed by Max.

Doc please tell me my kids are alright Zeek pleaded barely consolable at this point. the doctor placed a hand on his shoulder and said: they'll be fine, they just need some food and some rest right now. That son of yours withstood a lot of torture for his little sister and should be rewarded when he wakes up. Your little princess has some bruising around her ribs and a punctured lung, she'll have a scar from us fixing the puncture. The three men were in shock looking at the doctor and saying in unison"So she's in surgery right now"?

Yes the doctor explained feeling bad for the shell of a man standing before him. Mr. Williams I promise you we'll do all we can for your children, I just hope they will find whoever did this to them. We found them alright Rashad exclaimed and they're going to pay for this when we get them back to tennessee. Thank You Doc.Lawson for all your help but can I see my son now Zeek asked? Of course, right this way Doc. Lawson answered with a nod of his head. He led the three men down a long hallway passing the O.R. where Camille was in surgery at the moment and onto the elevator. On the 4th floor of the hospital in room 245 Christian was resting peacefully.

The sight of his baby boy in this sterile room battered and bruised looking lifeless broke Zeek's heart. Falling to his knees Zeek found himself praying the same prayer Mrs. Wilson said over him when he was 2. This time asking for his son to be spared and not taken away from him. All three of the men took a seat around the young man's bed to wait for any signs of life to come from him, then they each drifted off to sleep. Just as the sun began to rise Christian opened his eyes to see his dad and uncles still asleep. The young man weakly called out: Dad, uncle Max, uncle Rashad where is Camille? Is she alive? Did those ladies hurt her? The three men looked at each other then back at Christian with questions on the tip of their tongues.

6

Extended Hospital Stay

Max asked Christian with urgency: When the lady took you and Camille out of the house, was there anyone else in the car? No; it was just us but she was on the phone with someone saying she'd meet them at the warehouse, Christian answered. What happened when you got to the warehouse nephew, Rashad asked. When we got there another lady was there and she tied us up and Camille started crying. I asked the lady to untie me so I could calm my sister down and the lady that took us hit Camille. I tried to fight for my sister, I'm sorry dad I failed then Christian began to cry.

Hey little man don't cry you did good , you're alive and so is your sister Zeek replied. Your sister is in surgery right now. She's hurt pretty bad but she'll be okay. The news only made Christian cry even harder and asking could he see his sister with his own eyes. Max told him to calm down and wait for the doctor to tell them when his sister is out of surgery. Christian calmed down and then asked could he have something to eat since his captors didn't feed them at all.

Rashad walked to the door and offered the get Christian anything he wanted to eat from the cafeteria.

I want a burger and fries just like I'd have at home with grandma Janette. A burger and fries it is nephew coming right up, then Rashad was gone toward the elevator. As he got off the elevator heading to the cafeteria his phone rang with a call from Regina. Hey pretty lady, what can I do for you on this stressful day? I'm so happy to hear from you baby, have you found the kids yet Regina asked. Yeah we got them but it's worse than we thought out here. Camille is in surgery right now and Christian just woke up and wants a burger and fries, so I'm headed to get that for him. Don't tell Kahlani anything, let her husband speak to her after we talk to the doctor. He's trying to get Camille airlifted back to Tennessee from North Carolina as we speak alright.

Alright I won't talk to the girls about this baby, but let me ask you one more question before we hang up. Go ahead, what's your question, pretty lady? Regina cautiously asked: Do you think they'll ask Christian to testify in court? I'm not sure but they might ask him, we'll have to wait and see what the state wants to do. Okay I miss you and I love you , see you when you get home baby Regina responds. I miss you and love you too. I'll stop by your house when we get back.

After getting Christian his food Rashad made his way back upstairs to room 245. As he entered the room the doctor was about to give them an update on Camille's condition. Rashad handed the food over to Christian before taking a seat to hear what the doctor had to say about Camille. Go ahead doc the floor is yours Zeek replied. The surgery went well for your little princess but she is on a ventilator until her lung can function on its own. I understand you're not from here so if you'd like we can arrange a transfer for her tomorrow morning when we release Christian if you like. All 3 of the men along with Christian shouted "YES" as their answer to the doctor's offer.

7

Finally Going Home

The next day after breakfast a nurse came in to help Christian bathe and get dressed but Zeek turned her away. After all, his son was almost 12 years old, he could bathe and get dressed by himself. Once Christian was ready he took his father by the hand and got on the elevator to go downstairs to leave. In the car the young man looked at his father and uncles with worry in his eyes about his sister. Dad, should we call Ma and tell her what's going on with Camille? I'll call her when we get your sister comfortable in her room at the hospital in Tennessee and make sure she doesn't have any complications.

After a 5 hour ride back to Richfield Zeek, Max and Rashad were tired and Christian was well rested from napping on the way home. They dropped him off at home and went back to World Tavern for Rashad and Max to get their cars. Then Zeek went to the hospital to check on his little princess. At the hospital the doctors' said that Camille is breathing better and they're just waiting for her to wake up. The news made Zeek the happiest father in the world. So he picked up his cell and called his wife to give her the rundown of what happened.

Hearing her phone ring Kahlani answered on the third ring after seeing it was Zeek. Filled with anxiety she asked: Where are you? What happened to the kids? Where is Camille? Is she with you? Did you catch Destiny? Just rambling on with all the things that have been on her mind. With a light chuckle Zeek answered her saying: Yes, we did catch Destiny and Melody along with the officer who helped them escape. I'm at the hospital right now and Camille is with me. She was beaten pretty bad just like Christian was. I had her airlifted from North Carolina Children's Hospital back here and I'm about to go talk to the doctor when I get off the phone. Stunned, Kahlani says: I'm on my way up there to see my baby.

That's fine baby I'll tell the doctor to wait for you to give us the news Ok. After getting off the phone Zeek went to get something to eat while waiting for his wife to arrive. Across town Kahlani got dressed and was about to leave when she got a close look at the injuries on Christian who was laying on the couch. Shocked by the sight of his bruises she asked him to tell her everything that happened to them. Kahlani was angry at what she heard Christian describe took place the 5 hours after they were taken from their home. After giving her son a hug she was out the door to go see her 11 month old baby girl.

Once at the hospital Kahlani ran to the information desk asking what room her daughter was in. Before the clerk could answer Zeek approached and took her by the hand saying: I'll take my wife up to see our daughter now. In the elevator she turned to Zeek and asked: how bad is it? I already saw Christian on my way out of the house and he told me everything. With both hands in his pockets and his head down all he could say in reply was"Yeah" and nod his head. Getting off the elevator both of them walked down to the nursery where the nurses were giving Camille a bath. Upon seeing the bruising on her baby girl caused Kahlani to breakdown.

Then the doctor came over to them to talk about Camille's condition since being transferred. Mr & Mrs Williams your little princess is doing much better and is breathing on her own. It's going to be awhile until the bruising will go away but other than that she should be able to go home today. We're just waiting for her to regain consciousness as you can see we've been feeding her through a tube until she wakes up. Two hours later Zeek and Kahlani sat holding hands praying for their baby girl to wake up. Just as they finished their prayer little Camille started to cry in her bed next to them. Kahlani turned to pick her up crying herself.

Calming her little princess down, Kahlani started to sing a lullaby to her to ease Camille's fears. Then Camille looked over and began to coo saying"da da" with her arms out in Zeek's direction. He smiled and took his little angel from his wife and gave her a kiss making her giggle. Kahlani folded her arms and shook her head at the scene before her. Then the doctor and nurse arrived to check on baby Camille and were greeted by dad and daughter all smiles playing peek-a-boo. The doctor asked if the parents wanted the nurse to get Camille dressed while they talked to the doctor but Kahlani declined her help saying: I'll dress her after we speak to the doctor. Then the nurse left the room to go see another patient on the floor.

Once everyone was gone Kahlani dressed her little princess and put her in the car seat. Zeek picked up the car seat and took his wife by the hand walking to the elevator to go home. Now in the car Kahlani turned to Zeek to ask a question that was on her heart. Husband, what should we do about your exes this time since prison couldn't hold them? Well, baby we will have to go back to court again but everything leading up to that you'll leave up to me. For right now you'll focus on the kids while I handle the legal issues, Zeek replied with finality in his voice. Then he drove his family home and went to get some sleep.

8

More Questions to be answered

The next day Zeek called Max and Rashad asking them to

meet him at the station. Once at the station. After slapping hands with both of his friends, both men asked how the kids were doing. They're doing good, they're just happy to be with each other. Not concerned about me and Lani one bit, I guess the 2 older ones are still blaming themselves for the kidnapping and Christian still thinks he didn't do enough to protect Camille.

So bro, where do you want to start with the questioning since we have 4 suspects this time around, Rashad asked. Let's start with our new suspect Jamal Reynolads, Zeek replied. Do you want us in there with you or do you want to do the questioning by yourself Max asked. Looking at both of his friends Zeek simply replied" we'll all go in there to question each of them". And off they went to get answers from Jamal, Roger, Destiny and Melody. When will people learn that messing with the family of Ezekiel Williams will get you nowhere in life.

Room #1) Sitting at the table chained to his seat Jamal Reynolds looked scared at the sight of Zeek and the other officers. After taking a seat the officers just shook their heads at the sight of one of their fellow officers in cuffs. Then it was question time starting with Max:1) Do you know how bad this looks on you? Rashad:2) Why did you help the two women escape? Zeek:3) Did you touch my children during this kidnapping? Max:4) did either of them offer you anything in exchange for helping them? Rashad:) What role did Roger play in this whole situation?

Jamal: Look I'll tell you like I told Mike when he tracked me down yesterday. I know how it looks for me and all of Law Enforcement. I helped them because they made it seem that you (Zeek) were keeping the kids away from them. I had no idea that the kids they took weren't theirs at all. Zeek I never laid a hand on your children until I checked their pulse when I arrived at the warehouse. Neither of the girls promised me anything I already got what I wanted from them before they escaped. As for Roger the girls asked me to take a letter to him regarding where they could lay low and that's where this whole thing started.

Then the three officers got up to stand when Jamal hit them with a curve ball they never saw coming. Jamal announces with a straight face: Both of them might be pregnant with my baby at this time. Zeek turned around in shock and asked: Did you just say that both of my baby mamas are carrying your children right now? Jamal didn't even blink when he looked up at Zeek and replied "Yes I Did".

Room 2) It was time to talk to Destiny about the case and get some answers. Once in the room and everyone was seated the show began. Starting with Zeek:1) What were you thinking to kidnap two children that weren't even yours. Max:2) Why would you keep in contact with Roger when there is no inmate to inmate mail allowed? Rashad:3) Do you think you could be pregnant by Reynolds right now? Zeek:4) What was the purpose of you kidnapping my kids and trying to kill them?

Destiny: Look I didn't plan on killing them, that was all Melody that beat them. All I wanted was to get your attention and get you to take me back. The one thing we both had in common was that we want your wife out of the way. Since all of Roger's people are in jail thanks to you, we figured it couldn't hurt to ask Roger for help. Lastly; I have been feeling queasy so I think I could be pregnant. But how do you know I might be pregnant? Zeek replied with a straight face: Jamal told us when we talked to him. Destiny just put her head down and shed some crocodile tears that didn't faze the officers. Then it was now time to talk to Melody about her role in the case.

Room:3) Now it's time for some more answers from Melody

and maybe some understanding in this twisted tale of crime. Now that everyone was seated it was time to start talking and fast before Zeek loses his mind. Zeek:1) So you thought kidnapping and killing my children would make me take you back? Max:2) How did you manage to let Destiny talk you into this mess? Rashad:3) Have you been feeling under the weather lately? Zeek told her: Lastly You know the chances of you getting out of this are slim to none at this point.

Melody: Zeek we both thought that if we killed those kids and your wife that you'd only pay attention to us only. I didn't let Destiny talk me into anything, I wanted my baby daddy as much as she did. Since you asked I have been a little nauseous these last 2 days. And yes Zeek i'm aware that my chances of getting out of this is slim to none.

Prison(visit room)#1 Roger walked in again to see his son along with 2 other officers with serious looks on their faces sitting at the table. Then it was time for questioning and some much needed answers for the last time. Zeek got right down to business with the questioning starting with 1) Why did you help them with the kidnapping of my children? Max:2) Didn't you know inmates can't have any contact whether it be letters, phone calls, visits etc. Rashad:3) What was the arrangement between you and the girls about their mission?

Roger: With a smile on his lips he looked at the officer and began his explanation. The arrangement was that I give them somewhere to lay low from the cops and they'd bring my granddaughter to me for a private visit. I chose to help them because they promised to put money on my books once they got custody of my grandchildren. Yes I know that inmates can't communicate from the inside with one another. That's where Jamal came into play, he relayed the information between us via word of mouth and letters.

After hearing all of this information in one day filled Zeek with sensory overload. All he could do was shake his head and walk out followed by Max and Rashad. In the hallway the three officers looked at one another mentally drained after speaking to these deranged people. You should go home and get some rest man, Rashad told Zeek who looked like he was about to pass out from exhaustion. Yeah man you should really go do that, we'll get the case notes to Judge Anthony and the D.A. for you, Max replied.

9

Another Court Trial

Thanks guys I appreciate you doing that for me, you're right I really am tired of this crap taking place in my life. I'll talk to y'all later and call me if there are any new updates alright. We got you bro both of the men said before parting ways for the day. Once he got home Zeek headed straight to the shower and to bed for much needed rest. 4 hours later Kahlani came into the bedroom to check on him and Zeek was turning over in bed. Looking worried she sat next to him and held his hand asking how he was feeling? His reply was: baby I feel better physically but mentally I'm all over the place.

After having dinner with his family Zeek went to check on Christian and Camille. "Daddy" Camille shouted followed by Christian looking up from the dolls between him and Camille on the floor of her room. Zeek picked up his little princess and gave her a kiss on the cheek making her giggle. Then sat down on the floor with the two asking Christian how he was feeling. "I'm Ok" just wish I could have done more for us to stop this from happening. Son don't be so hard on yourself, you did a great job protecting yourself and your sister.

Looking over at his cheerful baby sister Christian smiled and felt much better about himself. That's when Zeek put Camille down and watched her run to her brother and wrap her arms around his neck which made Zeek smile. Just as he was about to go down stairs his cell phone rang with a call from Mike. I was calling to check on you so your mother wouldn't get a chance to harass you, Mike said with a chuckle. I'm good, and would be better once I get certain people out of my life. I would ask how you're doing but since you called before my mom I'd say you're still alive.

Yeah son I'm alive but some of those people you were speaking of won't be for long. What do you mean by that Mike? What took place while I was sleeping? Does my wife and mother know anything about it, Zeek asked curiously. Mike took a deep breath and said: Zeek you might want to talk to your lawyer and Judge Anthony about what's being said at the station. Thanks for the information Mike I'll talk to you later let me call down there and talk to the Chief. Then he called the station and asked Sandra if the Chief was in because he needed to speak to him now.

He's not in Zeek. Is there something I can help you with while I have you on the phone? No, I'll call him another time Sandy and again thanks for always being helpful everytime I call. Anytime Zeek, you know I got you Sandy replied before hanging up. The next call was to his lawyer to ask for a meeting with Judge Anthony. 2 hours later Zeek arrived at the courthouse to have his meeting. Walking into the Judge's chambers Zeek shook hands with the two men and took a seat. With a tired expression on his face Zeek asked: What's the next move with the case?

Judge Anthony adjusted his tie and nodded to Zeeks' lawyer to go ahead and explain. Well Zeek for his role Roger will be getting the death penalty, while Jamal will be brought up on aiding and abetting 2 fugitives. Melody and Destiny will be getting life with the possibility of parole in 25 years. Zeek nodded his head in approval of this news. Next, Judge Anthony said to Zeek there's one more thing you need to know about the case. The D.A. wants your son to testify against the girls and the abuse they sustained in the warehouse.

Zeek looked at Judge Anthony and replied: I'll talk to my wife and son about this but whatever it takes to keep my family safe is what we will do. So how much time do we have until we go to court? Well the first day of trial is in 2 weeks on Friday May 1st if you're ok with that Judge Anthony said looking Zeek in the eye. That's fine we'll be ready by then, see you then I'm going to let my family know about it, then he left heading to the precinct. Upon entry Zeek spotted Max talking to Mike in the lobby.

Hey;fellas I just came from talking to my lawyer and Judge Anthony Zeek informed. Really, what's the next step in the case Max inquired? In two weeks on May 1st is the first day of the trial and the state wants Christian to testify. In surprize both Max and Mike exclaimed: are you serious they want to put a child on the witness stand? Yeah man, that's the state's plan to make the conviction stick and move them to a supermax prison out of state, and Roger is getting the death penalty. We'll tell Rashad the news you head home and talk with your family, Max insisted.

I will be happy when this crap is over and my family is safe, so I'll talk to y'all later Zeek replied. Driving home Zeek kept replaying every part of his life in his head and couldn't believe the amount of evil surrounding him. As he entered the house he was greeted by his family with hugs. Zeek then took the hands of his wife and youngest son to have a talk about the trial. I need the two of you to understand something and don't overreact about it ok Zeek said slowly. Both Kahlani and Christian responded with: Ok what's going on that we need to know? I need the two of you to know that the court trial starts in 2 weeks and the state wants you to testify son.

Dad, what does that mean they want me to testify Christian asked? Before he could answer, Kahlani turned to Christian and held his hand to explain; it means they want you to tell the judge what the ladies did to you and Camille Ok. Do you think you can be brave enough to tell the truth in front of a lot of people in 2 weeks? So I have to miss a day of school to talk to those people then I get to come home and play with Camille, Christian exclaimed. Shaking his head Zeek replied "Yes" son that's exactly what we mean. With joy Christian stood up and shouted "I can do that" and went upstairs to play with his sister before bed,

Finally after 2 weeks it was May 1st and time to start what we hope is the last trial. Once everyone was sworn in and Judge Anthony was seated the state made their opening arguments followed by the defense. Then the state called Jamal Reynolds to testify against the girls. Jamal testified that he had relations with both of the defendants in exchange for helping them escape, with the promise being together once they regained custody of their children from Officer Williams. Then he told the court that it's possible that both of the defendants could be carrying his children at this time.

Hearing this information the entire courtroom was stunned into silence except for Zeek. Then it was time for the defense to cross-examine Jamal where he admitted to having started a relationship with Destiny a month before he started messing with Melody. It was at this point Reynolds realized that he'd been fooled by both of the women. Becoming increasingly angry Reynolds began shouting at the 2 women sitting at the defense table causing them to shiver in fear. Banging his gavel Judge Anthony told court officers to take Reynolds back to his cell.

Next the state asked for Christian to take a seat on the stand and the young man looked at his father for reassurance before leaving the gallery with the bailiff. Once on the stand the state asked Christian to detail his time with the defendants for the court.

Christian: It was quiet in the house after Harmony put Camille in bed for the night. Then I heard a knock at the door as I went to the stairs. I saw Malcolm going to get the door so I went back to bed. Then I heard a thud from downstairs and when I peaked out my room I saw Harmony going toward the stairs so I went into Camille's room to hide. Then there was a slam of a door so I thought everything was OK, so I opened the door to go back to my room and she was standing in the hallway.

Prosecutor: Who was in the hallway Christian? Can you point that person out for the court?

Christian: She's right there next to the man at the table across from the Judge

Prosecutor: Which one of the ladies did you see in the hallway

Christian: It was inmate AZ42809516 who walked into the

room and picked up Camille and said" hurry up let's go little boy" and dragged me down the stairs. As we were leaving I saw Malcolm laying bloody on the floor by the couch. I was worried and wanted to know what happened and where Harmony was. She pushed me and Camille into the back of a car, I couldn't see what type of car it was because it was dark and I was sleepy.

Prosecutor: Thank you Christian ; your witness Council

Defense: Christian can you tell us what happened after you left your house that night?

Christian: She took us for a long ride so me and Camille went to sleep but I heard her on the phone with someone

Defense: What did you hear her say on the phone?

Christian: She said "Mel I got the two younger ones" we're on our way to you now. See you in a couple hours at the warehouse.

Defense: what happened when you got to the warehouse?

Christian: When we got there the other lady told her to put us on the floor. So she tied us to a pole in the middle of the floor next to a heater. Camille was crying and I asked them to sit her in my lap and they said no. I told them she might be hungry and asked if they had something to feed Camille. The two of them laughed in my face and walked away. I got as close as I could to my little sister to calm her down and she laid on my leg letting her sleepiness takeover. I don't know how long we were asleep when they hit me in the head and the sound of Camille crying next to me. The lady that took us started yelling at Camille to shut up which made her cry more, then the other lady started to hit my sister in the chest and stomach. With tears in his eyes Christian looked at his father before he continued. Zeek gave his son a head nod to continue while wiping the emotion from his own eyes. Then Kahlani and the prosecutor gave him a nod to finish telling the story. Lastly: Christian looked at Judge Anthony who was also wiping emotion from his eyes, told the young man "go ahead son" he said.

Christian: I tried to get over to my sister to comfort her but then they started beating me and telling me not to move. At that point I just wanted to die because it hurt so bad. But I had to protect my little sister from those ladies. So I pleaded with them to leave her alone and just punish me. The last thing I heard before I passed out was them saying: All Zeek had to do was wait for us to come back to him and raise our children as a family. Since he took that option off the table for us, we'll take away his two babies and then we'll take away his wife .

After hearing this statement from a 9 year old child how was the defense ever going to win their case. The attorney knew his case was a loss at this point. No way was Judge Anthony going to ignore any of the evidence in the case, especially the testimony of Christian Williams. After Christian went back to his seat with his parents, Judge Anthony said: we'll reconvene tomorrow for sentencing, court is adjourned for today.

10

Conclusion of the trial

The next day Zeek and Kahlani left the kids home with Janette as they prepared for the sentencing. At Richfield County Courthouse reporters were asking Zeek what he thought the outcome of the case would be. Zeek replied "no comment" to all their questions and led his wife into the courthouse. Once seated Judge Anthony came into the courtroom followed by all the defendants and jury. Both sides gave their opening statements then took a seat to wait for the Judge to proceed.

Judge Anthony looked out into the gallery and made eye contact with Zeek and Kahlani. He proceeded to say: Jury, are you ready to deliberate this case? followed by the foreperson saying"Yes your honor". After the jury left Judge Anthony cleared his throat and with emotion in his eyes looking at each of the defendants. He then said: Each of you have done despicable things to Officer Williams and his family. Stooping to the levels of lunacy that have been spoken of in my courtroom are heartbreaking to say the least. With that being said Mr & Mrs Williams I offer you my most sincere apologies for what you have had to endure at the hands of the defendants.

After the jury returned from deliberating the foreperson stood to hand the verdict to the bailiff. Judge Anthony looked over to the jury asking did they come to a cohesive agreement on the verdict? Yes; Your Honor we have says the foreperson before taking his seat. The bailiff handed the envelope to the Judge and went back to taking his place next to the defense table. Judge Anthony took a quick look at the verdict and closed the envelope.

Then Judge Anthony asked both of the attorneys if they had anything else to present before he read the verdict? Lastly Judge Anthony asked Zeek and Kahlani if they had anything they wanted to say to the court, to which they both shook their heads "No". At this point in the case since all parties have nothing further to bring before the court, I'll go ahead with reading the verdict, Judge Anthony stated.

Jamal Reynolds on the charge of Aiding & Abetting the fugitives the court sentences you to 15 years and an additional

5 years for Sexual Misconduct.Melody Stanton you are sentenced to 10 years for Child Abduction as well as 25 years for escaping from prison, along with 10 years for premeditated murder of Kahlani Williams. Destiny Richardson the court sentences you to 10 years for the assault of Malcolm Williams and 15 years for kidnapping along with 25 years for escaping from prison. Lastly; both you and Ms. Stanton will be receiving 5 years for the bodily injury to Christian and Camille Williams. Both of you ladies will be moved to a supermax prison so we don't have to revisit this case again. As we know Roger Williams is on Death Row and for his role in aiding Ms Stanton and Ms Richardson his death by lethal injection will be taking place in 6 months from today on Nov 1st. Court is adjourned. Have a good day everyone.

11

Getting life back to normal

Once Zeek and Kahlani got home all of their children greeted them in the living room. After sharing the good news with the kids and Janette the couple went upstairs to relax. Janette stayed downstairs in the kitchen making dinner for the family. Zeek and Kahlani took a shower and laid across the bed to rest until Harmony knocked on the door with Camille in her arms letting them know dinner was ready. At the table everyone was surprised to see Michael sitting next to Janette holding hands.

After saying grace Michael leaned over to whisper in Janette's ear making her smile. Grandma what you got going on over there, Christian asked? Yeah Ma, What are you two up to over there Zeek asked curiously. Since y'all being so nosey I'll tell you "Michael and I are moving in together". I'll still come over to help with the kids while you two are at work and Malcolm goes off to College. You can rent out the house next door after I move my stuff out in two weeks. Then the family enjoyed their dinner before calling it a night. Kahlani helped Janette wash and put away the dishes while congratulating her on finding someone to be happy with.

Once Michael and Janette went home Kahlani made her way upstairs to check on the kids. All of them were in bed so she made her way to the master bedroom to call it a night. There was her handsome husband sleeping soundly, so she tiptoed into the bathroom to brush her teeth before getting into bed. Zeek turned over to greet his wife with open arms and that megawatt smile. Kahlani gave him a kiss and wrapped her arms around him saying:Good night husband. With a light chuckle Zeek responded: Good night wife.

Before she fell into a deep sleep she whispered to Zeek: I think we need to get Christian some therapy soon. He's holding Camille like something will happen to her if she sleeps anywhere else in the house. He won't even let me put her in her own bed. Before I left his room he told me that we'll need to have another baby in order for him to let her go. At that Zeek laughed replying: I'll talk to him in the morning baby, go on to sleep.

The next morning in the kitchen Zeek took Christian to the

side and asked him"what's going on with you man"? Dad I feel like I let the family down and didn't protect her. It makes me feel like something will happen to her again if I let her out of my sight. Even when I'm at school I want to run away to get back to Camille. Then Malcolm walked over and mentioned he felt the same way after being hit in the head by Destiny. After hearing both of his sons' concerns Zeek looked up at Kahlani with sad eyes. Then he told the boys they were going to have a men's day with Rashad, Max and Michael.

Malcolm and Christian thought this was a good idea but asked, where will Camille be? With a smile Zeek replied: she'll be with Harmony, Grandma, Mom, Regina and Cora for a girls day. After breakfast everyone went their separate ways for some time apart. The ladies went to the spa, Karaoke, The Mall, a dance studio for Harmony to sign up for a class. On the other side of town the men went to play basketball, eat lunch and then to a therapist's office where Zeek and his sons vented their feelings out.

After leaving the therapist's office the men met with the ladies at "World Tavern" for dinner. At the table both of her brothers covered Camille with kisses on each side of her high chair. While she was full of smiles in her high chair Kahlani and

Harmony felt so proud they started to cry tears of joy. Then everyone told each other what they had done the whole day. After the ladies spoke of their fun filled day the men told them about their day. Upon hearing that her husband and 2 sons had to see a therapist made Kahlani's heart swell. Then she asked if they could go as a family to one of the sessions?

Christian looked up at his father with hope in his eyes asking: Can they dad ? Sure son I see no reason why they can't go with us . After dinner was over everyone made their way home for the night. Before going to bed Zeek took a walk down to Christian's room where he found his baby boy holding his little sister as they slept. Zeek didn't think what his wife told him the night before was true until this very moment. When he tried to take Camille to her bed Christian started to shout "NO" to which Zeek left the 2 siblings entangled in each other's embrace.

Walking into his room Zeek locked eyes with his wife and sighed with a slight chuckle telling Kahlani what happened when trying to take Camille from Christian. With a laugh Kahlani asked Zeek what they should do about this child? Zeek replied: maybe we should try this family therapy thing here at the house. Kahlani agreed with the idea and told Zeek that she's so thankful to have him and these children in her life. Once ready for bed the husband and wife allowed their tiredness to take effect.

12

Family Therapy

The following week The Williams Family gathered together in their living room. After 15 minutes the doorbell rang and Zeek answered it welcoming Dr. Reva Matthews to his home. Then introduced Harmony and Kahlani to the doctor before proceeding. Each person is given the chance to speak before the doctor gives her response to what she's heard. She begins by saying: it's clear that each of you have endured some level of trauma in your lives and it's affecting your ability to move past it.

(You) Zeek have been conditioned to hide your emotions in order to protect and serve the public. (You) Kahlani are unable to feel comfortable anywhere in the world due to the childhood trauma you've endured. And with that you some days don't feel safe or loved if you're apart from the people in this room. (You) Malcolm feel that as a man and older brother failed your siblings in regards to the kidnapping last month.. And then there's (You) Christian who feels you didn't do enough to protect your baby sister during the kidnapping last month. So after speaking Dr. Matthews looked over to Harmony who was sitting with Camille playing in her lap off to the side. How does everything said today make you feel as part of this family?

Harmony spoke while handing Camille a toy saying: I feel sad hearing what you guys have on your conscience. Christian I think you were very brave through this whole ordeal. Mal you can't keep blaming yourself for what our moms planned to do to us. Dad, you and Ma never sat us down to tell us what grandpa did to you. Now knowing the story of your childhoods I'm deeply saddened by the news. In the end I think we can get past all of it with Dr. Matthews help. Oh! and Ma you've always been loved by us from the day we met you.

At this point Kahlani looked over at Dr.Matthews with tears in her eyes. Then she says: I've never heard anyone say that to me other than my mother. Next Kahlani walks over to Harmony and gives her a hug to which Camille reaches up in the air to be picked up. Harmony picks up a smiling Camille and gives her a kiss on the cheek. Then Dr.Matthews concluded the session asking the parents to let her know when they wanted to have another family session. Then she made her exit from the Williams home back to her office.

For the next 3 months the family continued to welcome Dr.Matthews into their home for their therapy sessions every other week. After every session each member of the Williams family felt like they were finally starting to overcome the trauma that has been holding them back . The whole family together went to watch Harmony in her dance competitions. When freshman tryouts for cheerleading came around they went to every game to watch her perform.

13

An execution and unexpected request from prison

On Oct 15,2020 a letter from the local prison came in the mail addressed to Zeek. In the letter were the details of Roger's impending execution coming up in 2 weeks, The warden asked if Zeek and/or Kahlani would be in attendance on Nov 1st. That night Zeek laid in the bed next to his wife and showed her the letter from the prison. So;Beautiful do you want to go or not because, I won't go if you're not comfortable with it. Wrapping her arms around his waist Kahlani looked up at Zeek replying:I think we should go to give ourselves closure and throw our trauma in the grave with him.

With a head nod and a quick kiss on her lips the answer was final. Zeek asked Michael to call the Warden at the men's prison to say both he and Kahlani will be at the execution of

Roger Williams. 2 days later another letter this time from the women's prison addressed to Zeek. Reading the letter Zeek's chest tightened after rereading the request asked of him and Kahlani. Seeing her husband in shock on the couch Kahlani sat beside him asking what's wrong?

Zeek handed the letter to his wife to see for herself and she also was surprised. The two women who plotted to kill her were asking for her to be a foster mother to their unborn children in 3 months from now. At the bottom it also states that they want them to watch the kids until Jamal Reynolds gets released in 5 years on parole.Why would they ask us of all people to look after their children?Then an idea hit Kahlani and she asked Zeek what he thought of her plan.

Babe since Melody's parents live across the street how about they take their grandbaby instead of us? Zeek, looking impressed by her idea,nodded his head in agreement. Next Kahlani asked if someone at the station could track down any of Destiny's family to take her baby as well? Zeek pulled out his phone, gave his wife a kiss and went outside to make a call. kahlani sat down on the couch still in shock holding the letter and couldn't believe what was happening in her life at this moment.

Outside on the porch Zeek called Rashad and Max on three-way to talk about what's taking place in his life.Are you serious man these two crazy girls want you to raise Reynolds kids until he gets out?Max asked, shocked. So what can we do to help Zeek?Rashad asked. Fellas I need you to do some digging to find anyone in Destiny's family that can take her baby in three months, Zeek replied.In unison the men said "sure man" we'll get right on it for you.

Two weeks later Nov 1, 2020 "The day of execution for Roger Elias Williams" was all over the news and radio. It was scheduled for 6am so Zeek and Kahlani asked for Janette to stay over and watch the kids until they returned. At the last minute Janette decided she wanted to go with them. But God was on their side because Ramona and Chef Jean were in town for a visit. Zeek drove his mother and wife to the prison arriving by 5:45 am.Entering the room to witness the execution there was a very cold aura lurking in the air.

Then the officers brought Roger in and laid him on the table strapping him down. With a creepy smile Roger looked up making eye contact with Kahlani who nudged her husband standing to her left. Then Roger's smile faltered seeing who was next to her replacing his smile with a scowl. The doctor came into the room and asked who were the people in the viewing room? The guard informed him that Roger's son, daughter-in-law and baby mama were viewing the execution. Then the doctor asked them if they had anything they wanted to say before the execution started? Zeek replied with an emphatic NO then looked at his wife and mother. Janette replied "Yes" as everyone turned to give her their attention . Janette then said: Roger you deserve what's about to happen to you today. You ruined the lives of me and our son as well as our daughter-in-law. If you ever had a heart you'd know that we could have been a happy family. For years I blamed myself for what you made me do but Zeek and Mrs.Wilson taught me that in **Ps 130:4 that with God is true forgiveness.**

I don't see how you can ever be forgiven in the eyes of the God I serve. You've let Satan control you for so long. I don't know where your soul is going after today but I know it's not going anywhere near either of us. Then they looked at Kahlani who replied: She said everything for us and you can proceed now doctor so I can get home to my kids. Then the doctor administered the sedative to Roger. Then the paralyzing muscle relaxer was administered to Roger. Lastly, Roger was administered the final sedative to stop his heart.

Roger never took his eyes off the three people whose lives he'd destroyed over the years. Then it was announced that Roger Elias Williams was dead at 6:45 am on Nov 1, 2020. The family of three stared into dead eyes that never blinked once during the execution. Once the doctor pulled the sheet over Roger's head Zeek took the hands of both the women beside him and walked out of the prison. Back at the house everyone was up and asking them how they were feeling after the execution. Since Zeek worked the night shift he went back to bed with no comment to the question. Malcolm took care of Camille since he didn't have to go to class until noon. And Kahlani went to get Harmony and Christian ready for school while Janette made breakfast.

14

New Discoveries

Over At the women's prison Destiny and Melody were separated until they were taken to medical. While waiting to be seen for their pregnancies Melody asked a question to Destiny. Did you really hurt my son when you went up into that house to get those two little kids? Destiny played innocent saying:I thought the one I took was yours not the one that opened the door when I knocked. In shock Melody asked: So you mean to tell me that you assaulted my child, the (oldest) of Zeek's children. The child I watched you play with on his third birthday across the street from my parents home.

My bad girl, it was a lapse in judgment that night please forgive me. Melody looked at the condition they were both in at this very moment. Here they are pregnant by the same man and due at the same time, while they were plotting to kill the same woman who'd stolen the heart of the one man they both wanted. Not to mention the fact that both of their children wanted nothing to do with either one of them and had a better relationship with the woman they despise.

In the men's prison Jamal was sitting in his cell when the CO came around. The Officer stopped at his cell and shook his head at Reynolds' appearance. You were such a good cop ,how'd you get yourself into a mess like this? Man, I don't even know how I let two broads get under my skin like this, Reynolds replied. Now I have two kids on the way that I won't get to meet until they are 5 yrs old. The CO continued on his way to check on the other inmates before going back to his desk. Jamal was kept in a separate cell away from the other inmates for his own security.

Zeek went to the station for his shift when Max approached him saying: bro I found some relatives of Destiny in Virginia. That's good to know man let me get that contact info maybe they'll be able to bond with Harmony also. I sure hope so man, here ya go good luck bro, then Max was gone. Before he could make a call Rashad came over asking how the execution was. Man it was like a horror movie playing out before my eyes. But I'm glad it's over and we all can sleep at night as well as walk the streets unafraid. What about the other three fools still rotting on the inside?

Zeek, I still can't believe they would ask you of all people after all the stress they put on your life, Rashad stated. What do you plan to do in regards to their kids? Are you going to adopt their kids for them? No, Melody's parents are going to take her kid once it's born. Max found some relatives of Destiny in Virginia that will take her kid when it's born. But I'm going to meet them first so they can get to know Harmony as well before the new baby comes.

Back at home after being at the station for a couple hours Zeek sat down with Kahlani and Harmony. He explained the fact that her mom was about to have a baby in 3 months. Then he asked Harmony if she wanted to go meet her moms family in Virginia? With a smile she said "Yes" and gave her father a hug and ran upstairs to her room. Zeek and Kahlani decided that they'd take all the kids with them to Virginia to give Harmony support. Three weeks later the family drove to Virginia for Thanksgiving weekend. Zeek and Malcolm split the driving that weekend, not letting Kahlani touch the steering wheel once.

15

Holiday Feast and New Beginnings

Once they arrived at the big colonial home just over the state line of Virginia, Harmony awoke excited. She took the lead in walking up to the door and ringing the bell. Once in the house everyone introduced themselves and sat down on the couch to talk. Christian was in the corner by the t.v. playing with Camille while answering every question asked of him. Destiny's Aunt Ella called everyone to the table for dinner where they said a prayer and dug in.

While eating, Aunt Ella volunteered to feed Camille for Zeek and Kahlani. They were very grateful but turned to her saying: You'll have to take that up with her brothers they're very protective of her since the kidnapping. Ella turned sorrow filled eyes to Malcolm and Christian who were getting kisses from Camille with sheer delight. Then she let them be and went back to her seat at the table to finish eating before dessert was served.

Once dessert was served Zeek decided to ask Ella how she felt about Destiny's actions as of late? With sad eyes she apologized to Zeek for having to raise Harmony by himself all these years. Telling him that she feels so bad for missing out on so many aspects of Harmony's life because of not knowing she even existed.I don't understand why Destiny wouldn't tell us about her pregnancy, it's not like we were going to shame her for it. Zeek didn't know what to say to Ella but he could understand how she felt. He asked himself the same questions when she left Harmony with him and disappeared.

After a fun weekend with extended family Zeek and Kahlani took their bunch back to Tennessee. Two weeks later Kahlani decided to make a trip to the doctor's office after getting all the kids' yearly exams done. The doctor and nurse both came in to do the exam and Kahlani was nervous but certain she knew the test results already. Dr. Swanson looked at her with a smirk and replied" Congratulations Mrs. Williams" you're expecting again.

With a bashful smile Kahlani nodded her head in acknowledgement then asked ,how far along am I doc? Based on your test results it seems you're 6 weeks along. Do you want to know what you're having this time around, nurse Jaime asked? Sure I'd love to know what I'm having but could you put a copy of the results in this envelope for me? Of Course, Mrs. Williams, I will gladly do that for you. With that being said it appears you are having "TWINS".

Looking up at the ultrasound screen Kahlani asked can you tell the gender of the twins right now? Dr.Swanson looked down at Kahlani with a smile replying: I sure can Mrs. Williams. Nurse Jamie reached down to help Kahlani sit up from the table and held her hand looking up at the screen. Dr. Swanson pointed at the screen saying: over here on the left is your little boy and on the right he paused for effect. Then he announces that your little girl is laying in her brother's arms. Before leaving he gave Kahlani a printout circling both of the tiny people in the photo.

16

Delivery of New Arrivals

Once she got home Kahlani tried hard to hide her excitement from the family. After dinner Harmony asked Kahlani; Ma why are you glowing over there? Is there something you and dad aren't telling us? Zeek looked over confused because he didn't even know what was going on. With a chuckle Kahlani handed her husband the manilla envelope with a wink. Baby last time you handed me one of these envelopes you were pregnant what is this about this time?

Open it and find out husband was all she said with a sly smile before stepping aside. Zeek stood between Malcolm and Harmony as he opened the envelope while Christian held Kahlani's hand. As he pulled the paper out Zeek gasped in surprise as he read it. The bold letters read: **You are 6 weeks pregnant with Twins.** In shock Zeek walked over and kissed his wife passionately. Christian asked out of curiosity: are they boys or girls? Kahlani took the ultrasound picture out of her purse showing it to everyone pointing out the circles. Over here on the left is your baby brother and he's holding your baby sister.

All of the children were overjoyed by the news but no one was as excited as Zeek. The emotion in his eyes led him to call his mother and his friends with the news. With her over the top self Janette asked Michael to bring her over to the house the next day. Walking up to the porch Michael knocked on the door just as Harmony came to open it. She was headed to get the mail just as they arrived to celebrate the good news. In the living room everyone was filled with laughter hearing Camille calling Michael"Pop Pop" repeatedly.

As Harmony walked in she was sorting the mail in her hands when she saw two letters from the Women's Prison addressed to her father. With apprehension Harmony gave the letters to her father and asked : what do they want from you now? I don't know princess but we'll find out now; Zeek replied. After opening the letter Zeek along with Kahlani and Harmony read the letter with him. The first letter was from the medical unit of the prison asking if he was going to come down and claim Melody's baby in February. Followed by the second letter asking the same request in regards to Destiny's child in the same month.

Dad, are you going to bring their children here with us in three months? I mean one is Mal's sibling while the other is my sibling, Harmony replied. Well baby girl Malcolm's sibling will be across the street with Mal's grandparents, and your sibling will be staying with Aunt Ella in Virginia. Then five months after that we'll be welcoming the twins into our home. I might have to call a contractor to attach our house to the house next door since your grandma moved in with Michael.

Okay daddy but will we get to see them some time, Harmony asked. Of course we will princess, we can go across the street to see Mal's sibling and we'll make a trip to see your sibling when you're out of school on vacation. That sounds good to me, daddy you are the best dad in the world. Oh and dad do we get to go to the doctor's appointments with ma or just you get to go? It's up to Lani who she wants to be there but most of the time it will be just me. We're not going to take you and Christian and Camille out of school during the school year unless necessary.

17

Three Months Later

By February 15th 2021 Kahlani was 5 months into her pregnancy and loving every moment of it. That husband of hers showed so much love and romance the day before. Since the doctor has her on bed rest for the remainder of her pregnancy with the twins. 7 am Breakfast in bed was fed to her followed by a walk in the park. 11 am lunch at World Tavern where everyone was just as excited about her pregnancy as she was. After dinner with the kids and some intimacy with Zeek, Kahlani needed a me day to relax.

Zeek paid a massage therapist to come to the house to take

care of his beautiful wife. When her massage was over and the therapist walked out the door Kahlani heard the phone ring. Upon answering the operator asked if Zeek was home to which she replied:No He's not I'm his wife, how can I help you? Ma'am I'm a doctor at the women's maximum security prison. Melody Stanton has given birth to a baby girl named Serenity Reynolds. She asked that your husband come pick up the child. Well my husband will not be picking up the child, Melody's parents will be picking up the child . Alright Mrs. Williams I will let the warden know this information. Have a nice day sir, Kahlani replied. You as well Ma'am the doctor answered before hanging up.

Just as she hung up Zeek walked into the house to find his wife sitting perplexed on the couch. Taking a seat beside her he asked: Baby what's wrong while placing his arm around her shoulders. Melody had her baby an hour ago and had the prison call here looking for you. What do they want with me Zeek asked? They wanted to know if you were going to come pick up the baby but I told them her parents were taking custody of the baby girl. Thank You for doing that baby and did she name the baby yet? Yeah, her name is Serenity Reynolds. I'm glad you said that because if she named the baby Williams I'd be headed down there to change that child's name right now.

With a laugh Kahlani replied: we'd both be down there husband. After sharing a laugh the two hung out with the kids for family movie night. Then two days later another call from the prison regarding Destiny Richardson giving birth to a baby boy named Harrison Reynolds. This time Zeek answered the phone while Lani was taking a nap. He informed the doctor that her Aunt Ella will be coming from Virginia to pick up the baby. After hanging up Zeek called Aunt Ella with the news and agreed to pay for her trip to and from the prison to Virginia.

Now he felt as if his life was finally Turning a new leaf in a good way. His father was out of his life and his family was expanding. His children were growing up fast before his eyes and a wife bringing him some more children. There's nothing more a man could ask for than this right here. Seeing his oldest go to College to join the same profession as himself. His second child is about to graduate from High School while his third child enters High School school. And his baby girl is going to Pre- School Not to mention the arrival of Twins.

His thoughts were interrupted by his mother Janette and

Michael ringing the doorbell. Welcoming them in with a hug and handshake Zeek asked what brought them there. Janette excitedly asked where Kahlani was because she had news to share with them both. At that moment Kahlani came down the stairs with 13 month old Camille in tow. What's the news Ma I'd love to hear it Kahlani stated. Well now that we're all in the room together I want to tell the two of you that "We're getting Married" showing off her ring. OMG I'm so happy for you Ma Kahlani stated happily.

I'm happy for you too Ma Zeek replied giving her a hug and kiss. Then he turned to Michael shaking his hand and saying: I'll be praying for you man. I don't know how you survived with her this long but I'm glad to see her happy. Then the phone rang again this time it was Ramona calling with some news of her own for everybody. Kahlani put the phone on speaker to hear Ramona announce that she and Chef Jean were also engaged. This family is growing in rapid succession everyday of the year.

By April 1st 2021 Malcolm came home from class with a young lady on his arm. Kahlani sat on the couch thinking this was a joke. Then Zeek and Harmony walked in asking: Who is this looking the girl up and down. Everybody, this is my girlfriend Kapri Smith. After a minute of complete stun each of them welcomed her with a hug. Then Zeek took his oldest child to the side for a talk. Son, be smart in this relationship game, don't do what I did with your mother. Don't let her convince you to take that condom off. And don't you ever pressure her to do anything she doesn't feel comfortable with. I know dad and I won't besides I'm not that type of guy, I'm every bit of you thru and thru.

18

New Young Love

Now that Malcolm has a girlfriend let's hope everything goes well for him and Kapri. Kahlani laid next to Zeek in bed and placed his hand on her abdomen with a smile. The babies decided they wanted to play, causing Zeek to kiss Lani's abdomen. So how do you feel about Mal having a girlfriend now? I'm happy for my son baby, but I don't want him to end up like me. I'll be disappointed if he ends up being a single dad like I was at 21.

I hear ya husband but you need to give yourself credit for being the best father to all three of those kids. You inspired Mal to go into Law Enforcement. That's a plus in the eyes of everyone around you. I'm so proud to be the person all of your offspring call mom. Now I also know this husband. I'll be having a conversation with Kapri very soon. And don't think I didn't see you in the corner talking to Mal earlier. The next thing we need to be concerned about is somebody showing up here talking about being Harmony's boyfriend ya know, then Lani was fast asleep.

The idea of some knucklehead boy trying anything with one

of his daughters made Zeek's blood boil. As a man, father and Officer it's his job to protect and serve but, his family comes first. Looking down at the sleeping beauty in his arms Zeek shook his head and went on to sleep. The next day there was a knock at the door just as the family finished breakfast. Harmony went to answer it with Camille right on her heels wanting to see who was there. On the other side of the door was Mr & Mrs Stanton holding their granddaughter.

Zeek and Kahlani walked over to greet them as they were amazed at how far along Kahlani was with the twins. How far along are you, Kahlani Mrs.Stanton asked? I'm 5 months and can't wait for it to be over so I can hold them. Wow, well anyhow we came over to see Malcolm and to let him see his sister. I'm sure he would if we could get him away from his girlfriend, Zeek said jokingly. Is he not home Mr. Stanton asked, turning toward the door? He's in his room studying. I don't think he'd mind taking a break. Kahlani hated yelling through her home so she texted Malcolm to come down.

Upon getting to the bottom step Malcolm noticed his grandparents standing at the door. Grandma, Grandpa, what brings you here? I would have come over to the house if you needed me to do something for you. Son, We don't need anything from you, we just wanted to bring your sister over to see you. Looking down at little Serenity's face Malcolm could see that she must have gotten her color from her dad. Her light complexion looked nothing like the rich melanin complexion of he and his other siblings. Even Camille was an even mix of milk chocolate from his dad and Kahlani.

Regardless, the little princess was another person for Malcolm to serve and protect. Just as he sat down holding Serenity Camille came over to see what he was holding. When she saw the new baby Camille got curious and tried to hold the baby with him. Zeek was impressed with Camille and explained that Camille is excited about her new siblings. Makes us wonder how involved she'll want to be with the twins in 4 months.

After they took Serenity back across the street to their home, the phone rang with a call from Aunt Ella. Harmony answered and heard the sound of a baby in the background crying. Who had a baby aunt Ella, Harmony asked in surprise? That's your baby brother Harrison. I picked him up from the prison after your mother gave birth. I was calling to arrange a weekend for you to visit with him. Is your dad or Kahlani home to make the arrangements with me?

Sure both of them are here I'll go get them for you Auntie, hold on . Zeek took the phone and greeted Ella before asking if everything was alright on her end. To which she replied: everything is fine I just wanted to make arrangements for Harmony to meet Harrison some time. That shouldn't be a problem since Kahlani is going to be giving birth to the twins in 4 months. OH MY GOODNESS, you're having twins maybe we could come over there and make it a family reunion . That's a great idea. I'll send you a train ticket and have my son Malcolm pick you two up .

I'm so happy for you guys and can't wait to see the munchkins in 4 months. After hanging up Ella looked down at the swing Harrison was sitting in and said: we'll be going to see your big sister soon little man. Back in Richfield Harmony sat down with Kahlani and her dad for answers that were on her heart. (1)Where was my mother anyway? (2) Who is the father? (3) Why hasn't she tried to be in my life? (4) Why'd she ask us to take Harrison instead of her family? (5) Why didn't she ask the father's family to take the baby?

Kahlani while rubbing her swollen belly answered first by saying: Your mother is in prison with Malcolm's mother

Melody. Zeek followed by saying:Harrison's father is Serenity's father as well. His name is Jamal Reynolds, he's one of my colleagues at the prison. I don't know why she hasn't been in your life all these years. But I do know that she kidnapped Christian and Camille to get my attention. She thought I'd give her custody of you if she took them. Kahlani then stated: She asked us to take Harrison so the two of you could grow up together without her and Jamal. She believed that her family would disown her for having a baby out of wedlock and that she also never told them about you. Zeek chimed in again saying: Uncle Max and Uncle Rashad are looking for Jamal's family to get them involved in the lives of Serenity and Harrison.

Okay daddy I hope they find them so the babies don't be like me finding their family after 15 years in the dark. Hearing Harmony's words made her parents' chests tighten not realizing how sad she's been her whole life. I wonder if she's talked to the therapist about these feelings, Kahlani said to Zeek. I hope so too babe, I've spent 15 years overcompensating for my kids not having a mother. Seeing his wife getting emotional Zeek turned to grab the bible on the coffee table.

Zeek called Harmony back downstairs to sit with them in the

living room. Baby girl after hearing your feelings on your mother I'd like you to read this scripture: **Ps 119:31** every time you get disappointed. Kahlani spoke up saying you can also take a look at **Rom 3:23 & Col 3:13** so you can forgive your mother for abandoning you all these years. Thanks ma and daddy this was helpful for me. Then she went back up to her room to read her bible.

19

More wedded bliss

A surprise visit from Ramona and Chef Jean at the end of the school year. As they arrived all of the family greeted them with open arms. After dinner and some conversation Janette asked out loud: How long do we have to wait for the news or are you two going to sit there looking suspicious? What do you mean by that Ma, Zeek asked curiously? It's obvious the two of them are in love and have been together for a while so when are you getting married like me and Michael?

With a smile Ramona looked up at Chef Jean who gave her a nod of approval. Then she looked at everyone and replied "We're getting Married" waving her left hand in the air. Excitedly everyone rejoiced with the two of them. Even Kahlani walked over to congratulate them before retiring to her room for some rest. Zeek helped her up the stairs, gave her a bath and tucked her into bed like a baby before going back down stairs. Once Zeek made sure his family was safe and his home was secure he went to bed for the night.

In the morning Kahlani had a doctor's appointment after taking Christian and Harmony to school. With Camille holding Zeek's hand the family walked into the lobby of Dr.Swanson's Office. After filling out her paperwork Kahlani sat with her family to wait. 15 minutes later a nurse came to usher them to the back. Dr. Swanson came into the room and greeted each of them, even little Camille, with a handshake. Then told Kahlani to hop onto the exam table.
Dr.Swanson picked up the wand after nurse Jamie put the gel on her stomach. Placing the wand on her stomach when the sound of the babies heartbeats appeared in the room. Everyone was excited, even Camille who pointed at the screen smiling. Then Zeek pointed to the screen saying: Babies as he looked back at Camille in his arms. After the exam was over the family

went to eat before going to get Harmony and Christian from school.

As soon as the family finished dinner Christian and Harmony asked Kahlani: Ma how do you feel about TuTu Wahine getting married? I'm happy for her guys really I am. I can't wait to plan it for her just like she did for me and your dad. Can we help too Ma, the kids replied happily to Kahlani? Next, Harmony asked what about Grandma and Michael getting married, do you think they'll have a double wedding?

They are best friends after all I don't see why not I'll ask when I speak to them again. How about we have a picnic in the park and invite them so we can pitch the idea to them before they leave town, Christian suggested. That's a great idea, little brother Harmony shouted looking at Kahlani. After some thought Kahlani said that would be a great idea and we can invite Ms. Cora and Ms. Regina. And Uncle Rashad and Uncle Max can come to hang out with dad, Christian announced. Yeah!!! little man, that's a great plan Kahlani stated with excitement.

Then it was time to plan the weekend picnic for the whole family. But first Kahlani needed to rest for a while before making preparations. After a two hour nap and a snack Kahlani was sitting in the living room when Zeek came into the house at the end of his shift. In shock she asked why he was home so early when he usually gets home just before dinner. Well I had called to check on you and my babies but nobody answered the phone so I came home. I can't have you going into labor while I'm at work and the kids are at school baby.

Your right about that husband and Camille wouldn't be able to call for help, Kahlani said with a laugh. Now I'm going to start dinner and try to figure out how to execute the kids' plan for a picnic on Saturday before our moms' leave town. I think it's a great idea as long as they're going to help you plan it, baby. You're not going to stress yourself out and nearly lose my babies doing all the work by yourself. The plan is that Harmony and Christian will be involved since it was their idea anyway.

That's an idea I can get behind so when are they going to start planning this so I can mediate the whole thing. We'll start planning tomorrow, I'm going to make enough food tonight for us to have leftovers to eat. I just hope everything goes well and everyone has a good time. Knowing my mother in law she'll be a comedy show by herself for no reason at all. But we'll see how everything turns out on Saturday. Shaking his head Zeek laughed thinking of how his mother cut up when preparing for his wedding to Kahlani. Yeah baby we'll see if she learned to behave as of late.

20

A Picnic and more surprises

Now Saturday comes and this 70 degree May 30th weather was perfect for a picnic. Zeek drove to Readman Park to set up for the arrival of the guests. Harmony and christian along with Malcolm and Kapri helped him unload the car. As Zeek and Malcolm were lighting the grill to start cooking and Kahlani and the girls were having some conversation at the table, their guests began to arrive. Starting with Max and Cora followed by Rashad and Regina then Ramona and Chef Jean followed by Michael and Janette.

All the men headed over to the grill where Zeek was with his sons. All the ladies gravitated to the table where Kahlani and Harmony were snacking with Camille on some food while talking to everyone. An hour later all the food was ready to eat so they sat down as a family to dine together. Kahlani looked over at Harmony who was just itching to ask the question that's been on her mind for the last 5 days. With a nod from Kahlani, Harmony asked: Grandma, since you and TuTu Wahine are friends and getting married, why not have a double wedding together.

Cora chimed in saying that's a great idea you should do it we are and couldn't be more excited for the big day. But you do what works for you ladies, I'm excited to plan my big day with my sister from another mister. Hearing this Janette and Ramona looked at one another and shrugged saying in unison"Why Not". Everybody was excited and ready to start planning even Camille was jumping with joy along with her two unborn siblings.

Kahlani winced in pain as the twins showed their approval of the celebration. Zeek ran to her side asking if she needed to call Dr.Swanson. Will they need to induce you right now? How far apart are the contractions? At that moment Kahlani felt a pop and shouted" my water just broke". Zeek picked her up heading for the car calling Christian to get Camille and come on. While everyone else was left to clean up before heading to the hospital.

Three hours later at 6:45pm The Williams Family welcomed 7lb 3oz Brandon Samuel and 6lb 8oz Ann Marie Williams. While Kahlani was resting Zeek took the family to the nursery to see the babies. Even the nurses were all filled with joy seeing those little cuties. When she woke up Kahlani wanted to see her babies first thing. That sweet husband of hers was sitting right by her bedside holding them which made her very happy.

Hi guys she said lazily watching Zeek coo with their babies. After spending time with the kids the doctor came to give Kahlani a check up and a clean bill of health then he stepped outside to let Zeek know that she could go home in two days. Ramona and Janette even chose to stay in town a little longer to help with the babies.

21

Planning (2) double weddings

Once at home Kahlani was greeted by her kids, mother and mother in law. After not working for nearly a year Kahani couldn't wait to go back to the workforce. First she had to enjoy her twins at home by herself. But really she isn't missing out on much since Cora and Regina keep her in the know of what's going on in the school system. The two of them are going to be around a lot since Lani will be helping with planning their weddings.

Now that Ramona and Janette are planning to stay in town to bond with their grandbabies and plan their weddings as well, Kahlani definitely will have her hands full. So, While the grandmas were enjoying the babies, Kahlani went into the kitchen to make bottles and lunch for everyone. Out of curiosity Kahlani had to ask them: Have you ladies chosen a date for the wedding? How about a location? Is it going to be in the states or a destination site? What are the colors for the wedding? Ramona replied:Lani relax we have chosen a date which will be June 30,2022. Janette replied: the location for the wedding will be in the Caribbean on the beach. I wanted the colors to be "black and burnt orange" but Ramona wanted"cream and baby blue" so I conceded and agreed with her choice. Kahlani smiled saying those are great options for the wedding. So what about the Caterer, florist, Music, Planner, the cake.

Ramona had only one reply on behalf of the two of them saying: We'll deal with that at a later date right now while we're in town. A dress is the main goal right now. Janette nodded in agreement saying: We made an appointment with the same dress shop you got your dress from. On Friday after Harmony and Camille get out of school we'll go. What about these two little cuties right here Ramona asked looking down at sleeping Brandon and AnnMarie.

They can stay with Malcolm and Christian until Zeek gets home,Janette replied. We can definitely do that and the girls will be so excited to participate. Before I forget let me ask you Janette are you going to be on your best behavior at the shop this time. Don't be extra like you were for my wedding planning. Ramona looked over at Janette curious as to what she's gotten herself into agreeing to this double wedding with her friend.

Then the phone rings and it's Regina with Cora on three-way. Kahlani puts the call on speaker for Ramona and Janette to hear so they can compare notes with the ladies.To start Regina announced that she and Cora agreed their wedding will be on May 28, 2023. Then Cora announced the colors will be "Red and White". Regina chimed in that the location of their wedding will be at The Egyptian Isles Resort off the Tennessee Coast.

Lastly before they hung up Regina says: Rashad and I

are going to be honeymooning in Paris followed by Cora saying:Max and I will be honeymooning in Italy. Next Ramona announced that she and Chef Jean will be spending their honeymoon moving into their new home in Hawaii. And Janette replied that she and Michael will be honeymooning in Mexico. While she was happy for all of them, Kahlani couldn't help but be sad that she and Zeek never had a honeymoon. Ramona noticed the sadness in her daughter's eyes saying: Lani why are you sad are you about to cry? Wanting to blame it on postpartum, Kahlani couldn't lie to her mother so she told the truth.

Mom; Zeek and I never had a honeymoon after both of our weddings. We never had any time away from the kids, we just got married and came home and conceived Camille. With his work schedule we only see each other at night for dinner then we go to bed. I never even got a chance to tell him where I wanted to go for a honeymoon. Then there was the mess with his dad and baby mamas harassing us nonstop. After hearing this Cora and Regina felt bad for their friend so they told

Ramona and Janette "We have to do something for them".

In agreement Janette and Ramona said in unison: lets meet up tomorrow to plan it out. Then they all hung up and Kahlani sat back looking at her newborns with emotion in her eyes. While she was alone with her children Kahlani thought about all the places she wanted to go for a honeymoon. Now that she had nothing to fear in terms of her children's safety and could breathe a sigh of relief. Zeek walked into the house breaking her thought process with a kiss.

Then he gave both of the twins a kiss asking her what was on her mind? Lani looked at him and replied: we never went on a honeymoon after both of our weddings. Perplexed Zeek stopped to think, saying: your right babe we sure didn't but, now that Malcolm, Harmony and Christian are older we can find time for a weekend getaway sometime. That's if you want to just say the word and we'll go wherever you want to go, do whatever you want to do. With a smile

Kahlani looked at her husband saying: I think our mother's are planning a honeymoon for us with the help of Cora and Regina.

22

much needed 2 week honeymoon

The following day Janette and Ramona met with Cora and Regina at World Tavern. While eating, each of the ladies gave their opinion on places that Zeek and Kahlani should go for their honeymoon. Regina suggested that they go to the beach. Cora suggested that they go to an Island. Janette suggested that they go on a road trip for 2 weeks. Ramona suggested that they go to a Hawaiian Island. Then Regina tells the ladies that they need to come to a decision.

So at this point the decision has to be made knowing Kahlani doesn't want to be too far from the twins. The best option for our favorite couple is going to a Beach Resort within the state, but which one. Regina shouted I've got it, how about we send them to "The Tahitian Shores Resort". It's 4 hours from their house and they won't have to be worried about the kids. Ramona had another idea saying: Janette how about we change our dress appointment to two weeks from Friday.

That's a great idea since we'll be in town to help with the kids while they're gone. Then we'll go dress shopping before we head back to the men of our dreams. Cora chimed in saying: you got that right girl, we know what you mean. Cora looked at Regina and said let's go get started on the reservation for our friends then turned to Ramona and Janette saying: you two go give our niece and nephew kisses for us. Then the ladies parted ways and focused on their tasks without letting Zeek and Kahlani know what's going on.

Just as they got to the house Janette received a text from

Cora with the reservation information. Smiling at each other the two moms were ready to set the plan into action. Walking into the kitchen the ladies went over to their children and told them that on Friday they needed to leave for their honeymoon. Kahlani was shocked by the news so she asked: what are you talking about? We just had twins we can't leave. In agreement with his wife Zeek looked skeptically at his mother and mother in law.

Hear us out Ramona says: You two have been married for 2 yrs and never went on a honeymoon. You got married, lived in fear for your family safety, and gave birth to 3 children. It's time for you two to have some quality time away from the kids, and that's why we're here now. Ma we haven't given any thought to where we'd even go for a honeymoon, Zeek replied. Don't worry we have it all covered son, Ramona responded; Cora and Regina helped us plan and pay for it.

Surprised, the couple looked at each other and smiled then hugged their mothers. So we leave in three days for two weeks alone but, we don't even know where we're going, Kahlani stated. You're going to The Tahitian Shores Resort. It's 4 hrs from here, Janette answered. That's the new resort on the coast; it has only been open for two yrs Kahlani proclaimed with excitement.

Three days later it was time for Mr &Mrs Williams to have their much needed honeymoon and rest. Once Kahlani got Harmony,Christian and Camille home from school she finished packing up. Can I go mommy Camille asked her mother with her puppy dog eyes. No babygirl you have to help take care of your brother and sister for us. Okay she replied feeling down as she went to her room to play before bed. After Zeek came in from work and had dinner and showered, the couple headed out.

Kahlani drove for 2 hrs so Zeek could rest for a while then he drove the rest of the way. Once they arrived and found their room the couple marveled at the beauty around them. Those cotton sheets on that California King bed were calling their names and they answered by getting under the comforter. After a good night's sleep the room's phone rang with a call from the front desk regarding their room service order. When their breakfast in bed was done the couple got dressed and headed out for the day.

23

Honeymoon activities and Homefield Surprize

As they approached the front desk the clerk gave them a list of activities to choose from. Knowing his wife the way he does Zeek walked Kahlani toward the spa. The couple had a facial, massage, and mani-pedi for the day. Lunch by the pool was next for the couple before heading back to their room. The husband and wife laid in bed to watch tv then took a nap before ordering dinner and calling it a night.

Sunday was a free day for them so they called in for their service meeting for 2 hrs. After being filled with God's word the couple talked about their marriage for the past 2 yrs. All the ups and downs and their hopes for the future along with Zeek's promise to always take care of her and their children. You know baby when we get back I have to train Mal out in the field.

Really; I'm glad he'll be with someone he can trust, I mean Rashad and Max would be good choices too. But to be trained by his father will be the highlight of his life. I guess you're right baby he has idolized me since he was 3. You know what I can't believe is that we have 1 child out of school, 1 about to graduate from high school, 1 starting high school, 1 in elementary school and 2 newborns, Kahlani replied. Yeah we did good raising some great kids, Zeek stated.

Speaking of kids, do you want anymore in say 2 yrs or when the twins start Kindergarten. Kahlani looked at her husband as if he had 2 heads raising her eyebrows in a stun. Then she replied" Heck No" fool didn't you hear me at the hospital after the twins were born. I told Dr. Swanson to give me a hysterectomy immediately. Laughing hysterically, Zeek responded, I remember now baby you were threatening the doctor and nurse.

You told them they'd be unemployed if they didn't prevent me from putting another baby in you. Laughing along with him Kahlani said" I meant every word and in that order too".

So; since you had a hysterectomy can I still enjoy my wife on our honeymoon? Looking shy Lani bit her bottom lip replying"of course you can Mr. Williams" as she raised the sheets to envite him to her side of the bed. Zeek with the sweetest of tenderness passionately kissed his wife while removing her nightgown. For the next 4 days they enjoyed all the couples activities at the resort. They even sat with other couples giving relationship advice to the other young couples. For another 4 days the couple took tours of the town with a local touring company.

Finally the last 3 days were spent in their room wrapped in each other's embrace. On Friday morning on their breakfast tray was a note from Harmony. Was she there with them? How did she get there without being seen? Who brought her 4 hrs to the resort? Kahlani curiously read the note and sat it back on the tray. She tried but failed terribly as she did at home when it came to not waking up her husband. Zeek turned over, reaching out an arm to pull Lani on top of him for a kiss.

Good Morning, Beautiful he said with a husky voice and after another peck she replied; Good Morning Handsome. As she turned to grab the food off the tray Zeek stopped her asking: What's wrong baby you look worried? Kahlani handed Zeek the note card off the tray to read for himself. Zeek's face turned serious as he read: **Daddy I hope you and mom are having a good time. I have something I want to talk to you guys about when you get home. I already talked to Malcolm about it and he wasn't too happy about it. Even TuTu Wahine and grandma Janette looked at me like I was crazy. I'll see you when you get home , Harmony.**

Turning to his wife Zeek said simply: Let's eat and get out of here. With a nod of her head she replied : We need to find out what's going on with her fast. I hope it's nothing drastic since neither of our mothers took the chance to discipline her. With that they finished eating and showered and made a BEELine for the elevator. As they passed the front desk the clerk asked if everything was Okay since they weren't due to check out until 1pm and it was currently 11am.

Kahlani stopped to tell the young lady that they enjoyed their stay but they have a family emergency and need to leave now. I'm sorry to hear that, and have a safe trip home, I hope you can come back with the family, the clerk stated sincerely. We'll definitely be coming back and thank you for giving us a great honeymoon experience. We will recommend this place to all of our friends, we'll even have our annual couples retreat here. That would mean so much to me if you did ma'am thank you so much the clerk cheered. Zeek pulled up in the car and Kahlani got in.

Zeek made the 4 hrs drive without stopping and didn't even let Lani drive at all. When they got to the house everyone greeted them with hugs and questions about their trip. After the two were settled they saw Brandon and Ann Marie in their swings in the living room next to a sleeping Janette on the couch. Zeek woke his mother up telling her she could go to Mike's house, and they'd take it from here .

24

Harmony's surprising news

Now that Malcolm is living in the house next door Zeek and Kahlani have an extra bedroom. Walking past that room was awkward after being so used to him growing up there. Across from his room was Harmony's room which Zeek stared at for a minute before knocking on the door. Come in, Harmony shouted through the door as her father entered. Standing at the foot of her bed Zeek calmly asked her to come downstairs to talk with Kahlani and himself then turned to exit.

Once the three were on the couch Kahlani looked at Harmony asking: What's this news you wanted to talk to us about? Well Mom and Dad I wanted to tell you guys that I was asked to prom by 2 boys at school. (1) Dametrius Little (2) Travion Smith. Dametrius is on the Basketball team and Travion is on the Varsity Football team. I also went on dates with each of them while you were out of town.

Surprised by Harmony's revelation both Zeek and Kahlani were at a loss for words. Now it made sense why Malcolm wasn't happy and the two grandmothers looked at her like she was crazy, because she certainly was at this point. Zeek then asked: (1)What did you do on these dates?(2)Where did they take you on these dates?(3)When did you get permission to go on dates with people we've never met?(4)How did you get to and from these dates?

Harmony started hesitantly by saying: I know you're going to be mad at me but please don't tell me I can't go to prom. Dametrius took me roller skating on Friday after you left for your trip. We talked about what color we'd wear to prom and ate snacks before getting dinner at Burger World. His mom was with us the whole time so nothing happened. Then on the next day his dad drove us to the mall to look at dresses and suits but we didn't buy anything.

Travion took me Bowling last Friday night and it was the same as before, we just talked about stuff going on around school and ate. His father was right there with us the whole time. I know I was wrong for making these choices without speaking to an adult first and I'm sorry. Zeek looked like he was going to explode listening to his daughter speak. Kahlani reached over to console him by rubbing his forearm then holding his hand. Next Kahlani said: we need to meet these parents before you can go to any prom or party.

Harmony picked up her phone and called Dametrius first, putting the call on speaker. When the call connected Harmony asked if his parents were home? Then she asked if one or both of them could come to the phone to speak with her parents? The young man called his mother to the phone and waited. When she came on the line Kahlani asked her if she could come over tomorrow to talk? Mrs. Little agreed and then they hung up.

Then it was time to call Travion to speak with his dad and the call was also placed on speaker. When the call connected Harmony asked if his dad was home to speak with her parents? Once his father got on the phone Zeek asked if he would be available tomorrow for a meeting? Mr.Smith agreed but said he couldn't stay long due to his work schedule. Now that everything is all set up the family went to bed for the night.

The next morning after breakfast Lani took Harmony to the side asking: Do you understand why we're doing this today? Kinda,Harmony said with a shaky voice. Well listen to me now young lady even if you have to record it on your phone. The last thing any parent wants is to see their child walk into a trap. I'm saying this because I walked into the trap of trusting a young man in high school. He promised to show me a good time but we didn't go to prom. He took me to me hotel and drugged me then he raped me while my arch rival and her friends held me against my will.

As a parent I'd hate to see my child go through the same things I experienced in high school. Do you know how many people are envious of you due to your association with me and aunt Cora? Every teenage girl and her mother wants to get in bed with your dad and they'll use you to lure him away from me and this family. Still to this day women still want me dead just to get their hands on your dad. This is why we are so concerned about your association with these young men.

Shocked by her mom's story Harmony just now realized how much potential danger she put herself into. Yeah, Ma I understand everything now and I'm sorry. For going behind you and dad's back making adult decisions on my own. Then the two ladies hugged one another just as the bell rang with the arrival of their guests.

25

Meeting the Parents and seeing an arch enemy

Harmony turned to answer the door as Zeek walked into the living room with the twins. Hi Dametrius, this is my mom and my dad. The young man extended his hand for a shake from both the parents saying:Mr and Mrs Williams it's nice to meet you. Then he turned saying this is my mom but was cut off by Kahlani. Danella when and how did you get out of prison was all Kahlani had to say. In surprise Dametrius looked between the two ladies saying: you two know each other, this just got weird.

Let's have a seat to talk inside Zeek stated calmly seeing his wife was about to explode. Once in the living room Danella noticed the twins in their swings with Camille sitting between them coloring. Mr. Williams, your children are beautiful, Danella replied, sauntering over to sit next to the swing. I think you should switch places with Harmony before my wife rips your head off. The sight of Kahlani with smoke coming out of her ears made Danella laugh. Just in a second the doorbell rang again with the arrival of the Smith Family. Kahlani went to answer the door coming back with Travion and his father.

Looking as if he'd seen an old friend Zeek shouted; Raymond Smith walking over to shake hands with the man. So now that we all know each other can we get this conversation over with Danella stated annoyed? Yes;Kahlani agreed, asking why would either of you allow your sons to go on dates with any girl without speaking to her parents first? I can admit I was wrong in the whole situation Zeek says, Raymond. We've known each other since the academy and when I used to bring this kid on ride alongs with us because I didn't have a sitter.

Wait a minute Zeek replied, you mean to tell me this is the same Trey that told us we were superheroes in his eyes. Raymond I trust you with my whole family. I just wish you would've called me when you noticed she was my daughter. Even Though I was on my honeymoon with my wife I still would have given the Okay. Now back to you Mrs.Little what was your reasoning for not acting like an adult in this situation? I had my mom bribe the parole board to let me out after 5 yrs on good behavior.

It's no secret this isn't my biological child, I adopted him and changed both of our names. I've been watching you live the life I always wanted and I got a plan. Once the kids were in High School I told him to keep an eye on her but your oldest child was always in the way. When he finally graduated I thought my plan could be executed but then this kid got in the way and showed up during their date stopping me from drugging her. In stunned silence, everyone looked at Travion with gratitude in their eyes.

In conclusion Zeek walked toward the two young men hugging Trey thanking him then turning with apologetic eyes on Dametrius saying: I'm sorry you had to be raised by such a horrible person son. Dametrius with his head hung low turned and headed for the door but was stopped by Harmony. I'll always be your friend and if you need to talk to someone I'm here to listen. He then nodded and walked on out of the door filled with sorrow. back in the house Harmony agreed to go to prom with Travion while her parents were coming up with a plan of what to do with Danella.

As she got up to leave Raymond slapped the cuffs on her and told Zeek: I'll be taking her down to booking for you. Before leaving Raymond also told Travion: stay here I'll be back to get you after I finish at the station. Zeek decided to leave with him to go to the station while Lani sat in the living room with the kids. Harmony decided to play matchmaker once again like she did for her parents. Travion and Kahlani looked confused as they watched her call her classmate Jazzlene who had a crush on Dametrius.

After asking Jazz to come over Harmony then called Dametrius to come back for a conversation. Within an hour both Dametrius and Jazzlene were in the living room looking confused. Harmony explained to them that they only had 4 weeks until Prom and the two of them needed a date so why not go together. The icing on the cake was when Jazz let Dametrius in on her secret crush she's had on him for the last 4 months. Dametrius was surprised and grateful for the truth and honesty that came from Jazz. Now that everyone was happy the two couples agreed to go shopping together.

Now it's time to get ready for prom so Cora, Regina and Kahlani took the girls shopping. While Zeek and Raymond took the boys to the tailor for their suits. All the men rallied around Dametrius seeing that he was still down after finding out what Danella was intending to have him do to Harmony. But on the upside he informed the guys that he and Jazzlene have made their relationship official. Congrats young man, we're glad to see you thriving in the face of adversity Zeek stated.

26

Prom and dating life

Now the day comes May 25,2021 "Prom Night" and the ladies looked exquisite in their dresses. Harmony in her Red Sequins Mermaid dress fit her shape to a T. Jazzlene chose an Emerald Green A-Line dress that made her shine bright. All the other students raved over the two young couples throughout the night. Zeek and Raymond were on security at the event for the protection of all the kids, not just their own.

After prom was over the two young couples got ready for graduation. That was a day full of smiles for everyone except Dametrius who had no family there to witness him get his scholarship to an Ivy League College. All four of the students decided to go to the same College. The first day of school and the girls chose to stay in an off campus apartment between the school and where Harmony grew up. The boys stayed on campus with the other athletes but they made sure to check on the girls everyday.One night two members of the basketball team along with two members of the football team tried to break into the girls' apartment. Thankfully Travion was in the area stopping by on his way home.

"Nobody is going to lay a hand on my girl" Travion thought as he parked his car in the lot. Just as he stepped out of his car the four guys saw him coming and tried to make it seem as if they came to check on the girls. The question is why are you here to check on "MY" girlfriend as well as Dametrius' girlfriend. That's my job so don't come back over here every again. Then the 4 men went on their way while Trey knocked on the door. Once Harmony came to the door and greeted him, he explained what happened and went into the apartment. He also explained it to Jazzlene so she would feel safe but instead she called Dametrius in fear for her safety.

Then she came back into the living room asking both Harmony and Trey"shouldn't we call your dads for help"? Harmony looked at Jazz shaking her head saying: not tonight but if they come back after Trey or Dame leaves for the night. OKaay;Jazz replied with a sigh as she went back to her room. After Harmony went to bed Trey left to go home but sat in his car to place a call to his dad and Zeek. After informing them of what happened at the girls' apartment both of the fathers told him to stay there until they arrived.

Trey gave them the names of all four of the young men who were trying to get into the girls' apartment before leaving. The next day all four of the young men were picked up for questioning by Zeek and Raymond. Each of the four men gave the same story that they were contracted by Danella to drug and rape Harmony and anyone in the apartment. In exchange she was going to have her husband pay them $2000 each when the job was done. When Kahlani heard this information she was a ticking time bomb as if what Danella did to her in high school wasn't enough she's now going after her child.

Two months later both Trey and Dametrius moved into an apartment closer to the girls. Once a week Malcolm comes by to check on the girls, followed by Zeek coming by once a week. Then Raymond comes by after going by the boys' apartment but the boys come by to check on the girls everyday. The two couples still go out on double dates for the girl's safety. They even asked Zeek and Kahlani if they could tag along on their group dates as well.

The couples sat back to observe the relationships of every couple in Zeek and Kahlani's inner circle. All of them were inspiring, especially Janette and Michael. Nobody knows how that man puts up with Janette throughout the planning of their wedding .

To Be Continued..............

We'll pick up from here in "The Golden Years" Book 4 in this series

Get ready for

- 2 weddings
- more group dates
- 4 honeymoons
- more of Janette's comic relief
- an introduction to Series #2 "Bonded By Love"

Milton Keynes UK
Ingram Content Group UK Ltd.
UKHW020120221024
449869UK00010B/360